AGATHA CHRISTIE

DEAD MAN'S FOLLY

Ruby
from
Mathew [signature]

BY MAREK

INTRODUCED BY MATHEW PRICHARD

GREENWA

HARPER

Agatha Christie, Greenway and Dead Man's Folly

Not many of Agatha Christie's novels are based specifically on real locations, but perhaps it is not surprising that two of them are in Devon, the county in the West of England where she was born, and where she spent family holidays regularly from the 1940s onwards. The first location was Burgh Island, an island off the South Coast, cut off by the high tide, and which gave rise to the idea of *And Then There Were None*; but most obvious was Greenway, on the River Dart, on which *Dead Man's Folly* is firmly based. Agatha Christie spent two months at Greenway virtually every summer from the time I was about four to the time she died in 1976. She did so at a time of year that she devoted to her family, in a part of England that had been close to her heart since her childhood. She loved its seclusion, the rambling walks down by the river, the old-fashioned grandeur of the house, and it was the ideal place to entertain her friends and family.

It was also, she discovered, an ideal place to set a murder mystery — we had flower shows and fêtes; Greenway had a boat house, secluded enough to conceal a body, and the atmosphere I remember is just the same as in the book, though fortunately in those days we experienced no crime!

Dead Man's Folly was written in 1956, a boom time for Agatha Christie and for Greenway. I think she would be delighted that over 50 years later, Greenway's charms are available for her many fans, particularly those who have come to appreciate her graphic novels.

Mathew Prichard
Grandson of Agatha Christie

HARPER
An imprint of HarperCollins*Publishers*
77-85 Fulham Palace Road
Hammersmith, London W6 8JB
www.harpercollins.co.uk

First published by HARPER 2012
1

Comic book edition published in France as *Poirot joue le jeu*
© 2011 Heupé SARL / Emmanuel Proust Éditions,
55, rue Traversière, 75012 Paris. www.epeditions.com
Based on *Dead Man's Folly* © 1956 by Agatha Christie Limited. All rights reserved.
AGATHA CHRISTIE®, POIROT® copyright © 2010 Agatha Christie Limited
www.agathchristie.com

Adapted and illustrated by Marek. Colour by Christophe Bouchard.
English edition edited by Thalia Suzuma.

ISBN 978-0-00-745133-3

Printed and bound in China by South China Printing Company Ltd.

POIROT HAD RECEIVED A PHONE CALL THAT MORNING FROM HIS FRIEND MRS OLIVER, THE DETECTIVE NOVELIST.

...There's a big fête thing here tomorrow and there's going to be a Murder Hunt. Arranged by me.

Half a crown to enter and you've got to find the Victim, and say Whodunnit and find the Motive... And there are prizes.

And you have sent for me to assist you in arranging this?

Oh, no! I wanted you for quite another reason.

I think there's something wrong.

If there was to be a real murder tomorrow instead of a fake one, I wouldn't be surprised.

A real murder?

I feel such a fool, not to be able to be more definite about it.

An intuition, some details...

Several people have made changes to my plot. I've felt jockeyed along.

There's the boathouse, where the Body's going to be.

And who is going to play the part of the Body?

We've finally settled on a girl from the village, a Girl Guide. Marlene Tucker, she's rather simple. Her role will be easy.

But come along now, we'll go back to the house and then you can meet everybody.

This Folly was only put up a year ago. Quite nice of its kind but why here? You can't see it stuck away in the midst of trees. Obstinate old fool!

MICHAEL WEYMAN WAS AN ECCENTRIC YOUNG ARCHITECT.

These tycoon fellows have no artistic sense.

2

Mrs Folliat... Monsieur Hercule Poirot.

What a beautiful spot!

Yes. The house was built by my husband's great-grandfather.

NASSE HOUSE HAD ONCE BELONGED TO MRS FOLLIAT'S FAMILY. BUT WHEN HER SONS HAD BEEN KILLED IN THE WAR, SHE HAD BEEN FORCED TO SELL THE HOUSE. SHE NOW LIVED IN WHAT USED TO BE THE LODGE.

It must be hard for you to have strangers living here.

So many things are hard, Monsieur Poirot.

3

George, this is Monsieur Poirot who has been kind enough to come and help us.

Sir George Stubbs.

We're so glad Mrs Oliver persuaded you to come. Quite a brain-wave on her part. You'll be an enormous attraction.

SIR GEORGE STUBBS OWNED THE HOUSE. EXTREMELY RICH, HE HAD BOUGHT HIMSELF HIS TITLE.

He's probably dead sharp in business, I should think, but frightfully stupid outside it.

Hattie!

4

Hattie!

Sorry I didn't hear you. How do you do?

Hattie is Lady Stubbs ... She's much younger, and definitely half-witted. Married him for his money, and doesn't think about anything but clothes and jewels.

This silly dispute about the tea tent has got to be settled, Jim.

MRS MASTERTON WAS MARRIED TO THE LOCAL M.P.

Oh, quite.

What about the fortune-telling tent? Should it go in front of the magnolia or at the far end of the lawn?

CAPTAIN WARBURTON WAS THE MASTERTONS' AGENT.

Not near the magnolia!

ALEX AND PEGGY LEGGE WERE FROM THE VILLAGE.

One needs to spread things out.

The coconut shy can't be too near the house. The boys are so wild when they throw...

And this is Miss Brewis.

MISS BREWIS WAS BOTH THE SECRETARY AND THE HOUSEKEEPER. SHE WAS KNOWN TO BE 'VERY GRIM AND EFFICIENT'.

I see you are all in a state of great activity.

There are always so many last-minute things to see to. I was on the phone half the morning, over marquees and tents...

... and the catering equipment...

A sandwich?

But perhaps you would rather have a cream cake?

What a very lovely ring!

George gave it to me yesterday.

He's very kind.

D'you see? It's winking at me!

HA HA HA

Hattie!

Devonshire is a very lovely county, don't you think?

Yes.

When it doesn't rain!

But there aren't any nightclubs.

You like nightclubs?

Oh yes, there is music and you dance. And all the women have nice clothes and jewels...

But not as nice as mine!

Perhaps, if I were not rich, I should look like Amanda...

She is very ugly, don't you think?

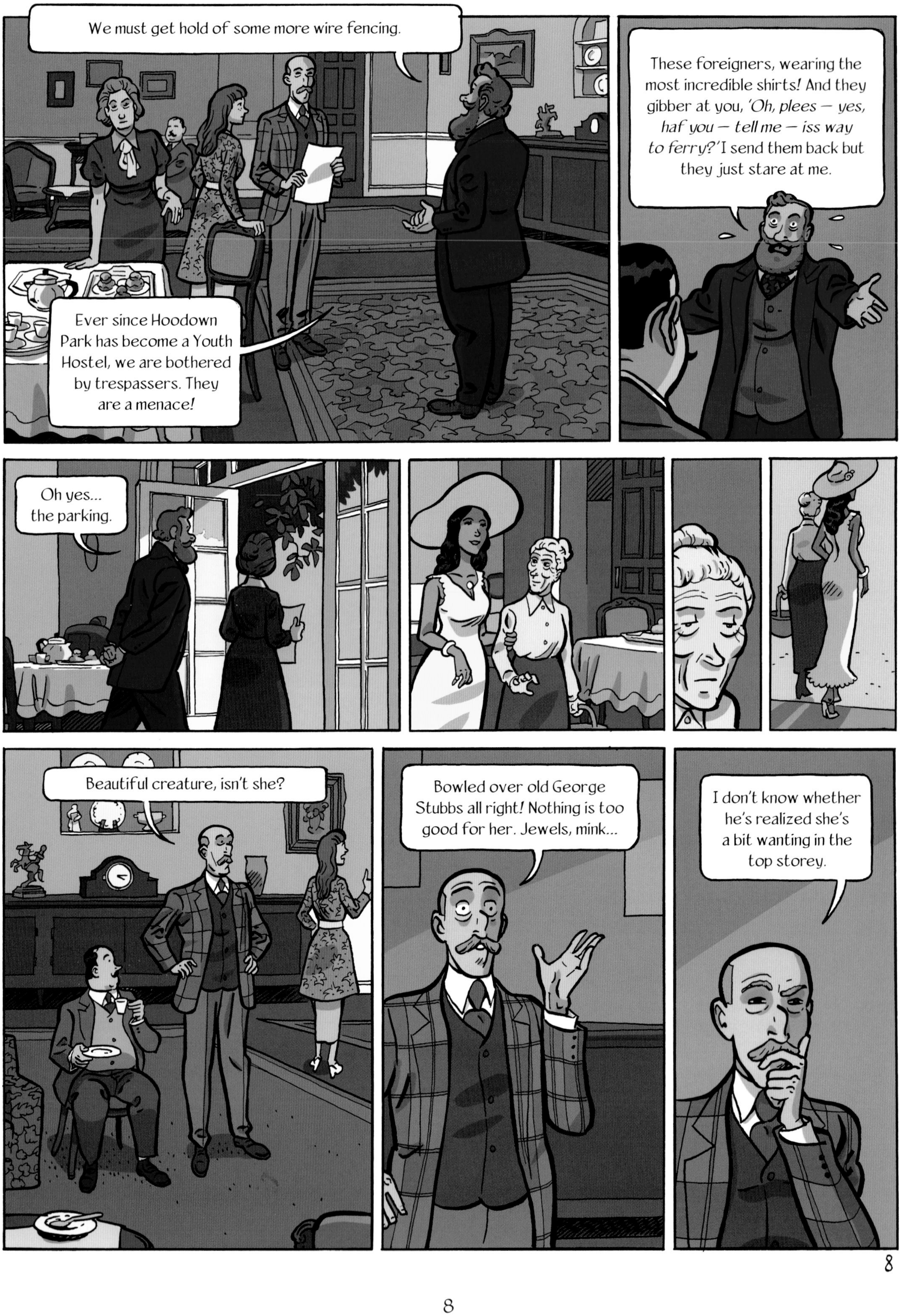
We must get hold of some more wire fencing.
Ever since Hoodown Park has become a Youth Hostel, we are bothered by trespassers. They are a menace!
These foreigners, wearing the most incredible shirts! And they gibber at you, *'Oh, plees — yes, haf you — tell me — iss way to ferry?'* I send them back but they just stare at me.
Oh yes... the parking.
Beautiful creature, isn't she?
Bowled over old George Stubbs all right! Nothing is too good for her. Jewels, mink...
I don't know whether he's realized she's a bit wanting in the top storey.
8

What nationality is Lady Stubbs?

I believe she comes from the West Indies, one of those islands with sugar and rum.

Please, Jim. The tent has to be in front of the rhododendrons!

Everyone will get one of these cards for writing down the clues. They will have to go from one clue to another, just like in a Treasure Hunt.

It's like this: Peter Gaye who's an Atom Scientist has married Joan Blunt, and his first wife's dead, but she isn't, and she turns up because she's a secret agent, or maybe she's just a hiker... This man Loyola turns up to spy on her and there's a blackmailing letter which might be from the housekeeper...

It sounds like a muddle, but when you see the synopsis leaflet it all becomes quite clear!

The only thing you have to do is present the prizes.

Well? Have you found out anything?

Everybody appears to be in a state of nervous agitation, which is characteristic of preparations of this kind.

9

I've been looking for you. Can I show you your room?

This is perfect.

Am I to congratulate you or my charming hostess?

Lady Stubbs spent her entire time being charming.

A very decorative woman, but in other ways is she lacking, perhaps...?

Lady Stubbs knows exactly what she's doing. Besides being very decorative as you say, she is also very shrewd.

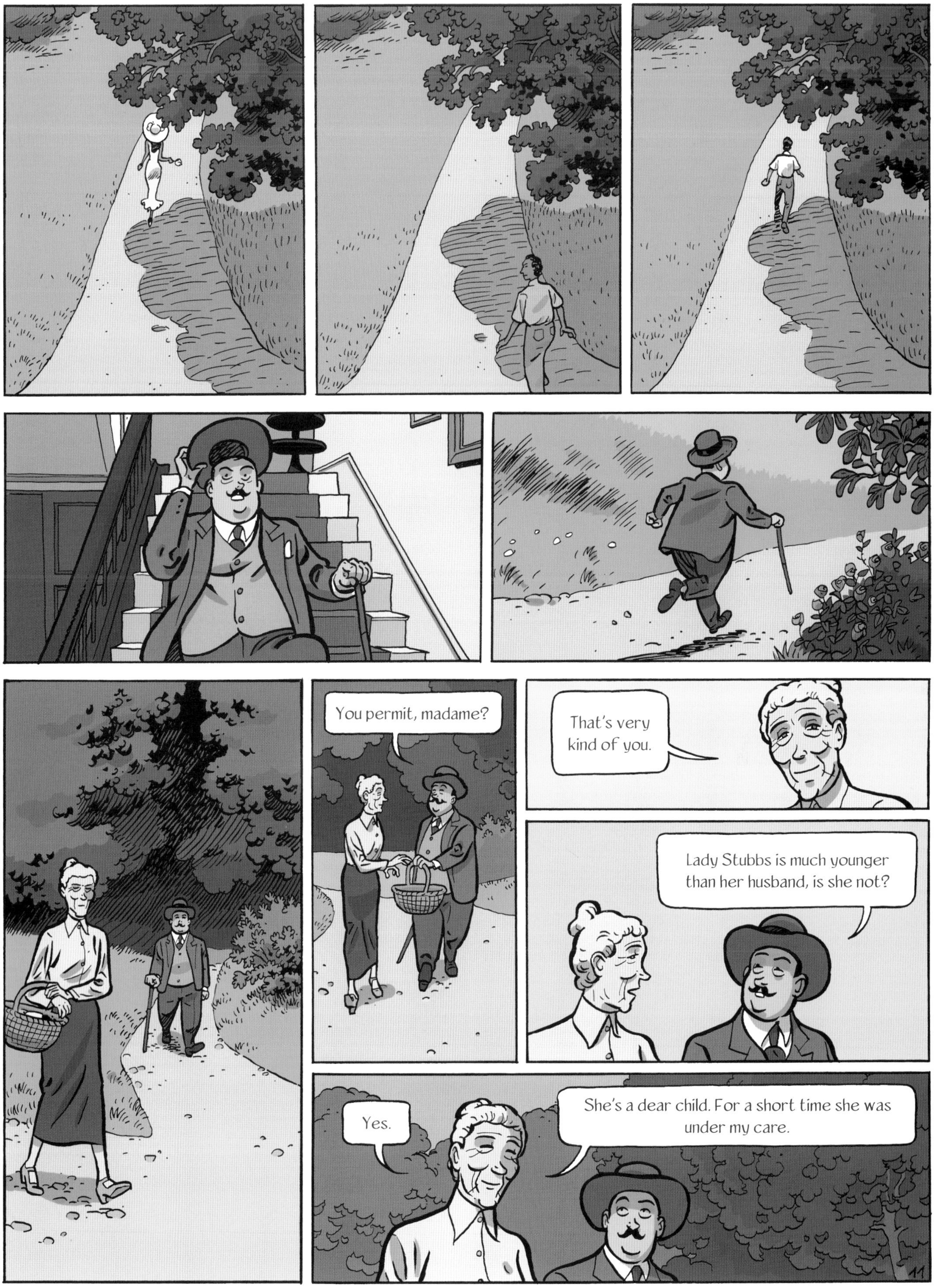
You permit, madame?
That's very kind of you.
Lady Stubbs is much younger than her husband, is she not?
Yes.
She's a dear child. For a short time she was under my care.

Her parents died in an earthquake and she suddenly found herself alone.

She had to be looked after and so I agreed to become her chaperone and introduce her into society. I had the necessary connections.

All this was after the war, after I'd lost my two sons.

I was thankful that a man such as Sir George Stubbs wanted to marry her and bought the house. Though he is a little vulgar, he is kind and decent.

And of course, he is very rich. I don't think he wanted intellectual companionship from a wife.

FERRY
DART CROSSING
Summer timetable:
Mon-Fri 6am to 10pm
Winter timetable:
Mon-Fri 8am to 3pm

Price: 6ᵈ

Ah, 'tis up at Nasse you are? Worked there as a boy, I did. And my son, he was head gardener there. I'm Merdell.

It must have been hard on Mrs Folliat to have lost both sons?

Ah, she's had a hard life, she have. Trouble with her husband and with the young gentleman, too. Not Mr Henry, but Mr James. He caused her a lot of trouble, but he died bravely in the war.

So now, there are no more Folliats at Nasse?

Don't ee never believe that, sir. Always be Folliats at Nasse.

What do you mean?

Mrs Folliat be living up at Lodge, bain't she?

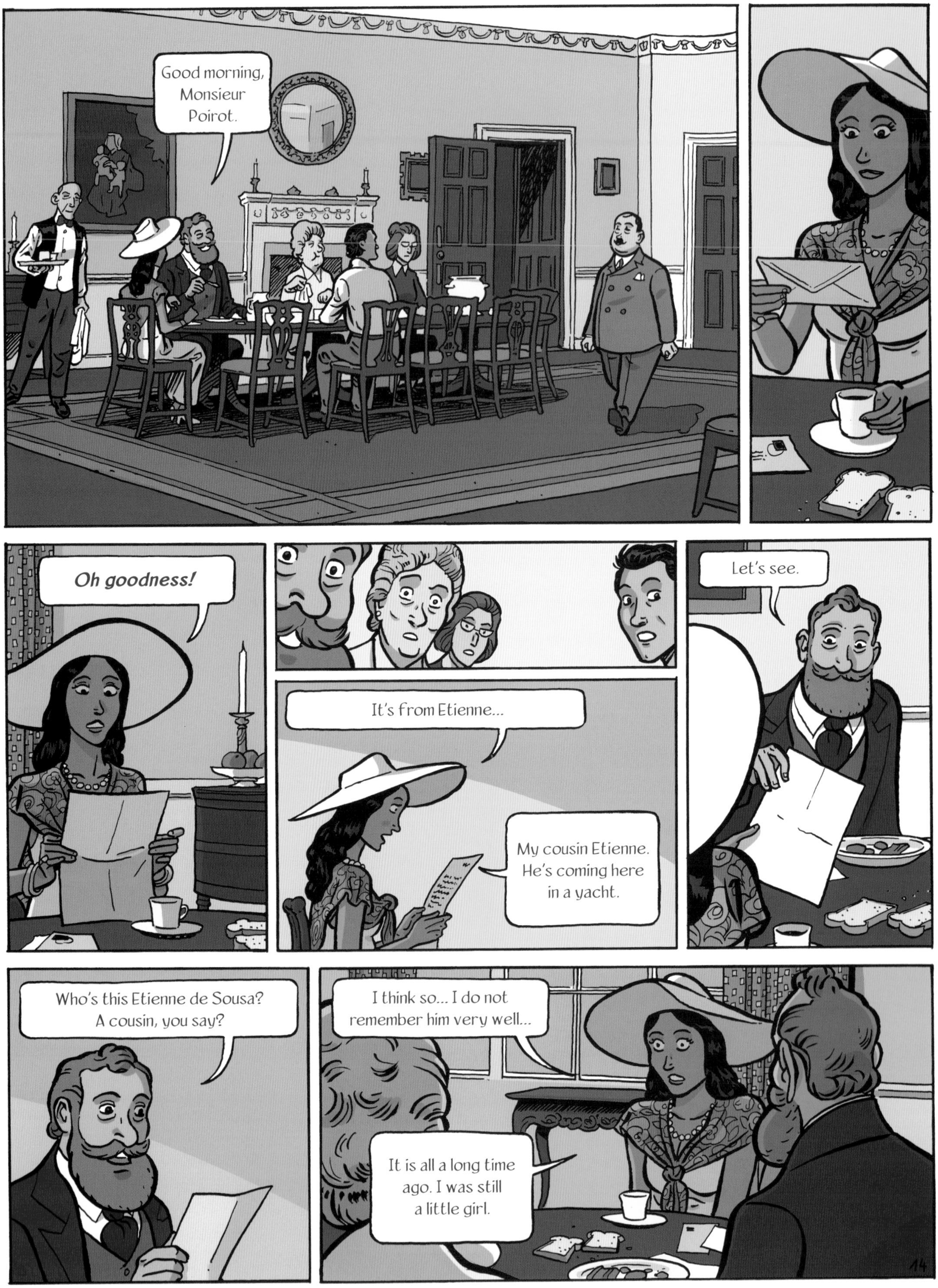
Good morning, Monsieur Poirot.
Oh goodness!
It's from Etienne...
My cousin Etienne. He's coming here in a yacht.
Let's see.
Who's this Etienne de Sousa? A cousin, you say?
I think so... I do not remember him very well...
It is all a long time ago. I was still a little girl.
14

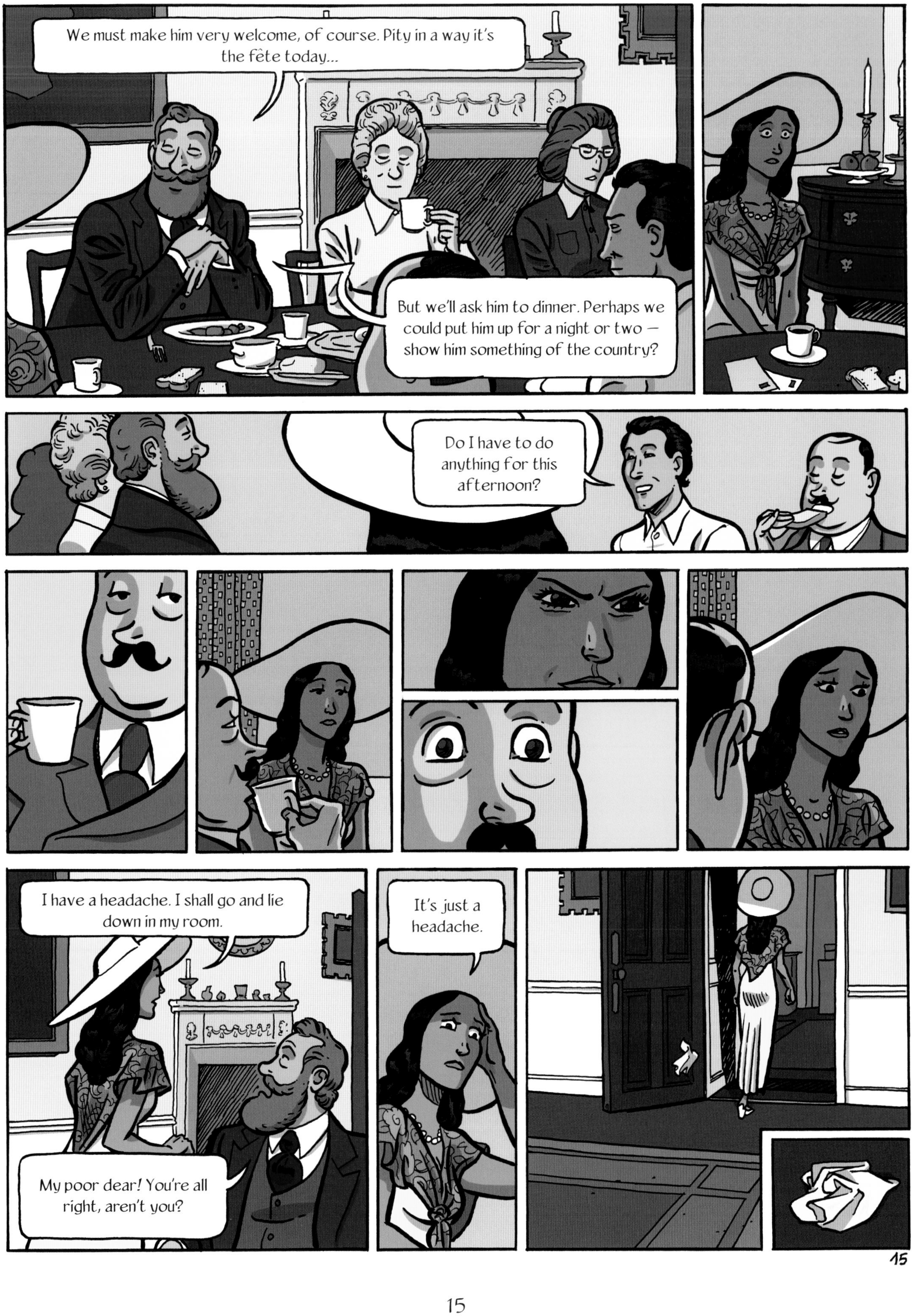
We must make him very welcome, of course. Pity in a way it's the fête today...
But we'll ask him to dinner. Perhaps we could put him up for a night or two — show him something of the country?
Do I have to do anything for this afternoon?
I have a headache. I shall go and lie down in my room.
My poor dear! You're all right, aren't you?
It's just a headache.
15

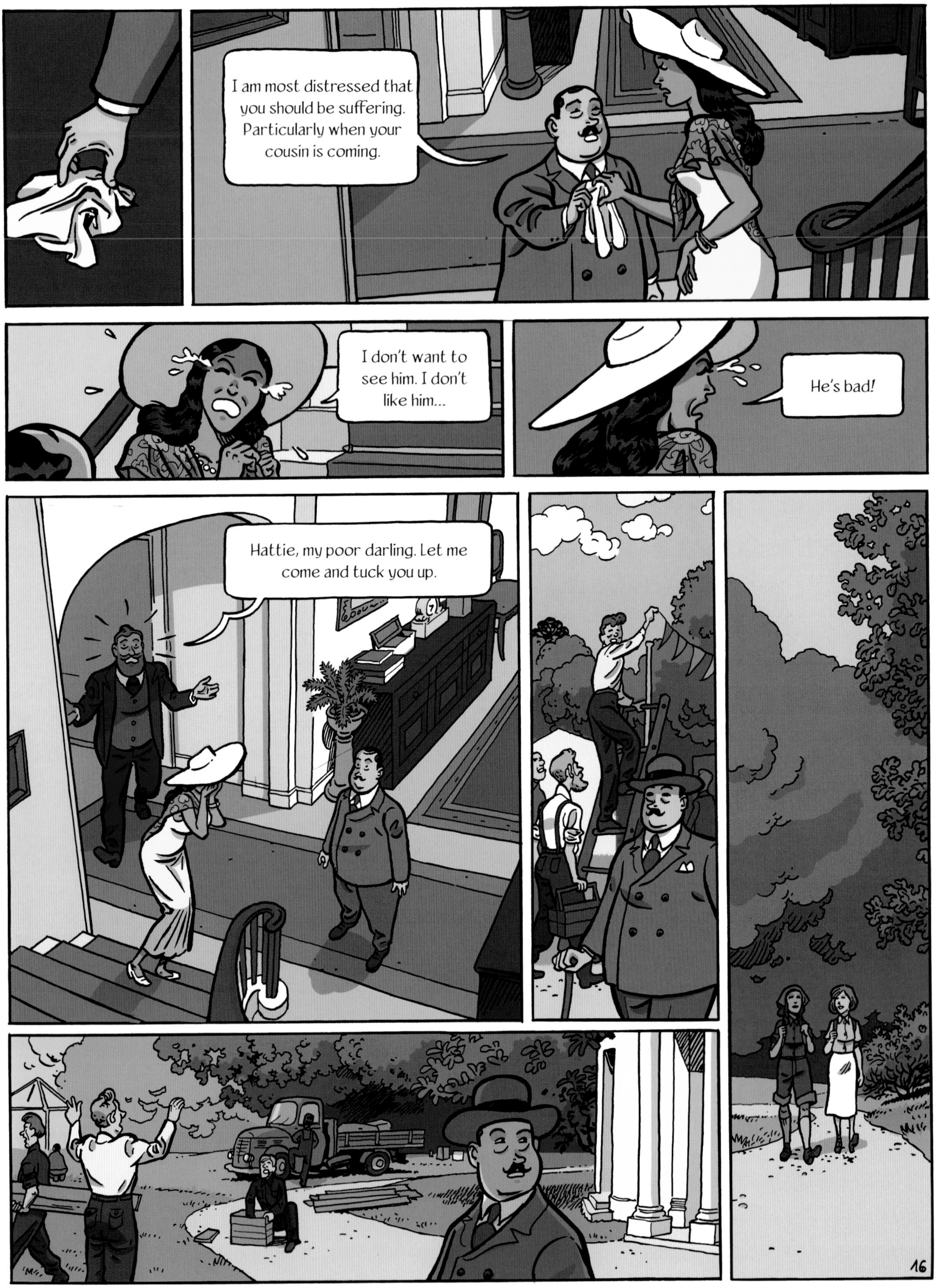
I am most distressed that you should be suffering. Particularly when your cousin is coming.
I don't want to see him. I don't like him...
He's bad!
Hattie, my poor darling. Let me come and tuck you up.
16

You're trespassing!

Please? Nassecombe Quay... Is it this way?

You can't come through here. It's *private!*

Spend all my time turning people away...

AFTER A QUICK LUNCH, EVERYBODY WAS READY.

PEOPLE WERE ARRIVING IN LARGE NUMBERS.

This is young Marlene Tucker.

So you're a real detective?

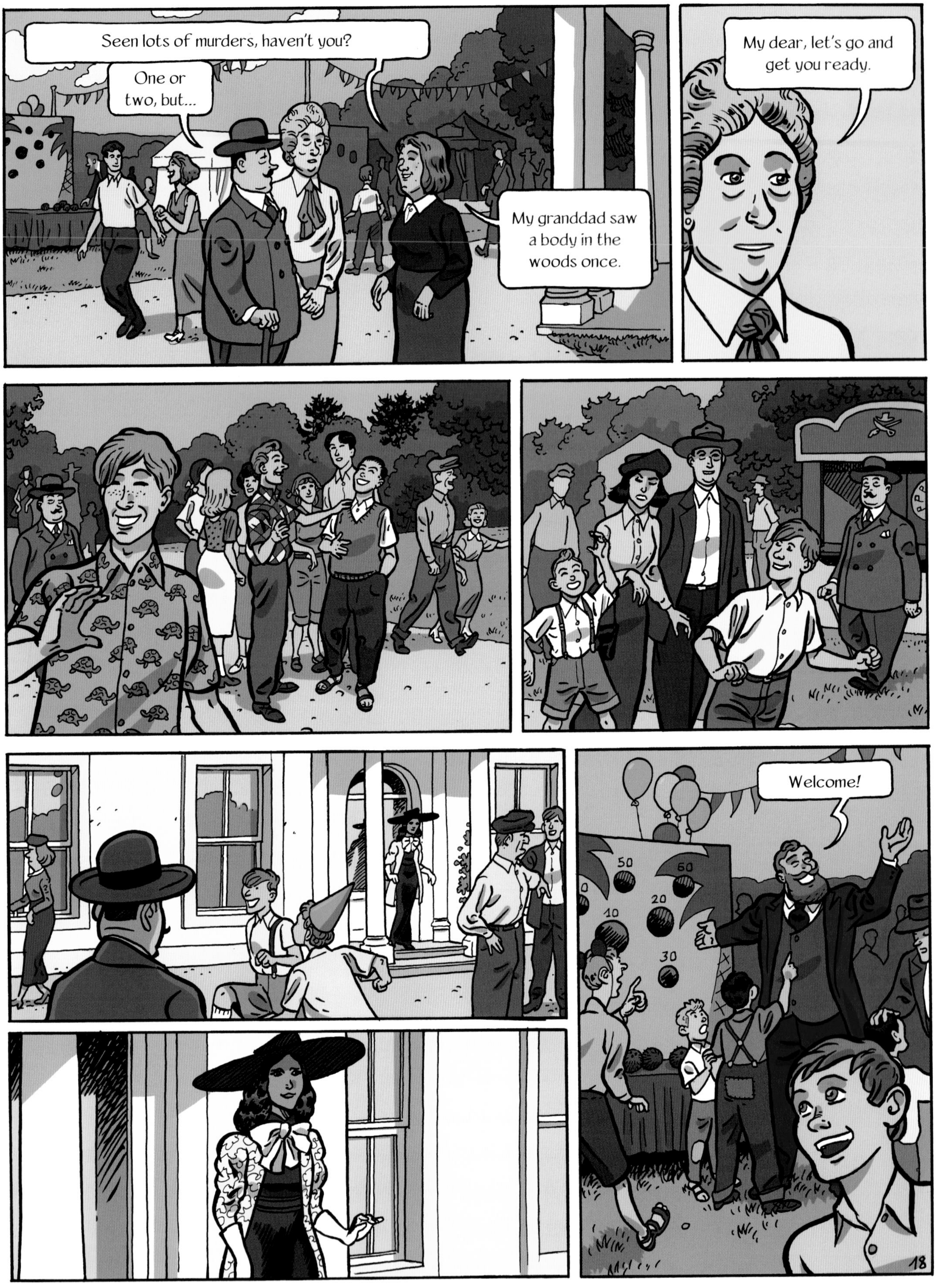
Seen lots of murders, haven't you?
One or two, but...
My granddad saw a body in the woods once.
My dear, let's go and get you ready.
Welcome!

Oh, Pamela, how nice of you to have come!

We felt we had to come and see Nasse in its glory.

Mrs Knapper, I am pleased to see you!

It's been such a long time.

Mrs Folliat has completely slipped into the role of the hostess...

Hello! I think that I'm in the lead!

The first clue was a weird photograph. But I spotted what it was, a section of a tennis net.

Now where does this one go, I wonder?

This next clue doesn't seem to make sense. You're not competing, are you?

Oh no, young man. Just observing.

...success with a dark beauty, plenty of money to come... and a miraculous escape from an accident!

Madame Legge, you are playing your role beautifully. I was told that you were originally to be the 'Victim'..

I wish I was being the Body. Much more peaceful. Actually, it's time for my tea break now.

Come on, sir. Come and guess the weight of this cake.

Well...

21

Have you seen Lady Stubbs? She's supposed to be judging this Fancy Dress business and I can't find her anywhere.

I saw her about half an hour ago.

Curse the woman. Where can she be? The children are waiting and we're behind schedule as it is.

Excuse me.

Is this the house of Sir George Stubbs?

I am Etienne De Sousa.

Hercule Poirot.

De Sousa? Delighted to see you. Hattie got your letter this morning. Are you staying here long?

Two or three days, it depends.

We must find Hattie. She ought to be judging the fancy dress.

I'll ask Miss Brewis. Excuse me a moment.

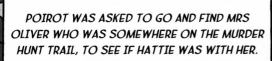

POIROT WAS ASKED TO GO AND FIND MRS OLIVER WHO WAS SOMEWHERE ON THE MURDER HUNT TRAIL, TO SEE IF HATTIE WAS WITH HER.

The Folly? Oh yes, that little temple.

Ah, Monsieur Poirot. This is only the second clue. I think I've made them too difficult. Nobody's come yet.

Patience, madame, and courage. The afternoon is still young.

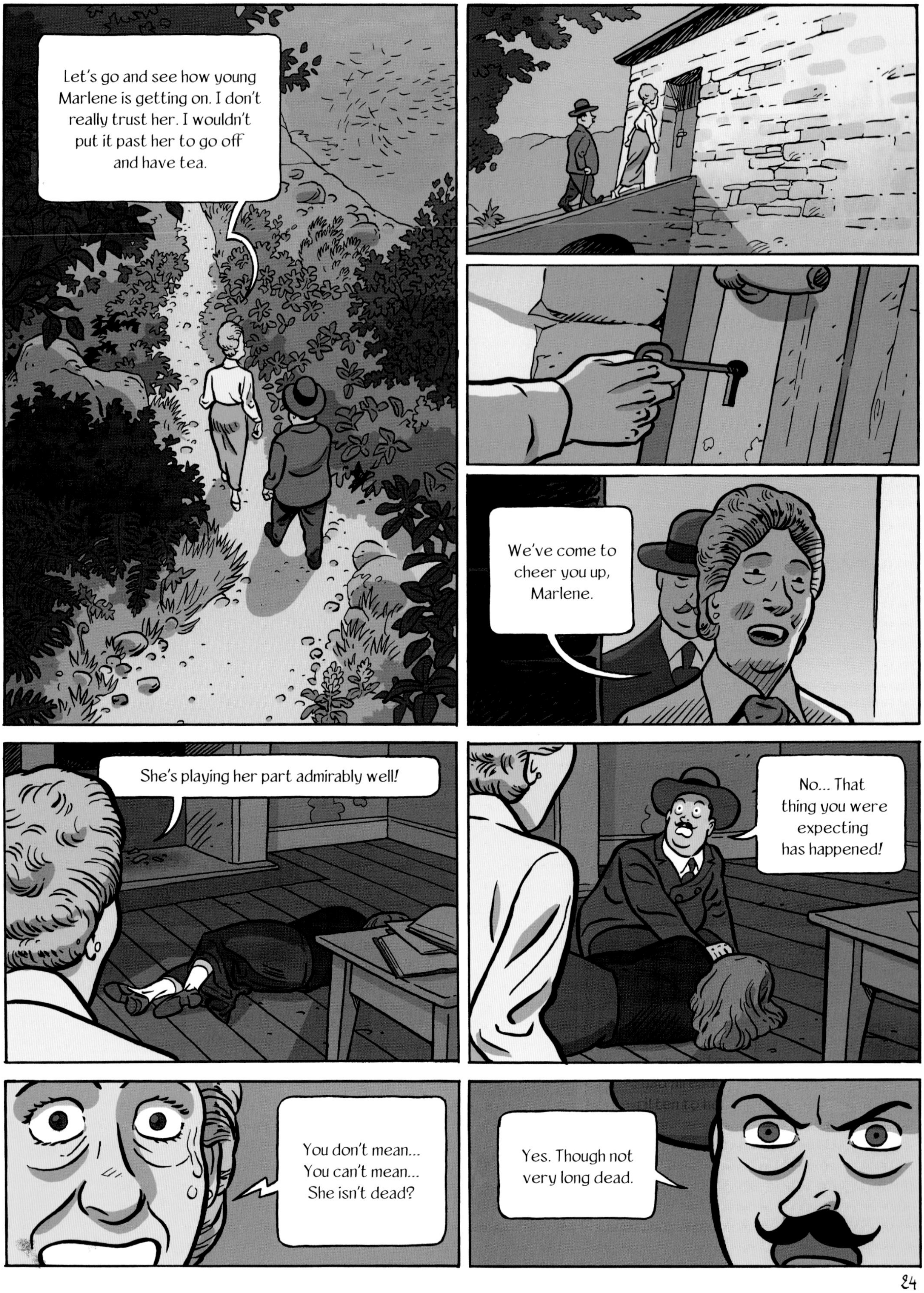
Let's go and see how young Marlene is getting on. I don't really trust her. I wouldn't put it past her to go off and have tea.
We've come to cheer you up, Marlene.
She's playing her part admirably well!
No... That thing you were expecting has happened!
You don't mean... You can't mean... She isn't dead?
Yes. Though not very long dead.
24

SIR GEORGE STUBBS HAD INSTALLED DETECTIVE-INSPECTOR BLAND IN THE STUDY.

There's a rumour that there's been an accident...

I don't think anyone has suspected yet that it's — well...

...murder.

How many people are there at this affair?

A couple of hundred, with more on their way... Unfortunately it's been a great success!

But I don't see why anyone would want to go murdering a girl like that.

The victim is an innocent young girl. I think the murderer must be a foreigner. Maybe one of those who stay at the Hostel.

25

I've finished the examination. The girl was garrotted with a piece of clothes line.

Bring in Miss Brewis.

At four o'clock Lady Stubbs told me to take a tray of cakes and a drink to Marlene.

And she was alive and well?

Yes of course. And very eager to know how people were getting on with the murder hunt.

MARLENE TUCKER'S MOTHER WAS SUMMONED TO THE INSPECTOR'S OFFICE.

I don't understand it at all...

Marlene sometimes had quarrels at school...

Words with her teacher sometimes...

But nothing serious, nobody who'd do her a mischief!

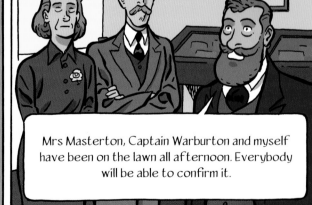

Mrs Masterton, Captain Warburton and myself have been on the lawn all afternoon. Everybody will be able to confirm it.

26

I feel awful. *Awful!* Because, you see, it's my murder. I *planned* it!

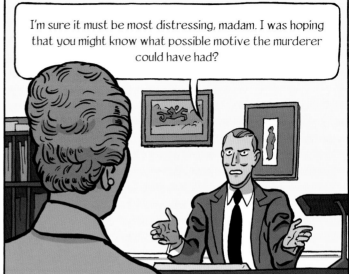

I'm sure it must be most distressing, madam. I was hoping that you might know what possible motive the murderer could have had?

Well, there are hundreds of possible motives! Marlene might have known some secret, or she may have recognized somebody who was concealing his identity, or a man in a boat may have thrown somebody into the river and she saw it from the boathouse... Or she may have got hold of a secret code...

What do you mean by the man in the boat?

Lady Stubbs' cousin, the one who came on his yacht. She got a letter from him and she was frightened.

Frightened? What of?

Of him. Anybody could see it. I think that's why she's hiding now.

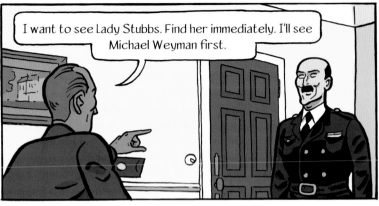

I want to see Lady Stubbs. Find her immediately. I'll see Michael Weyman first.

According to a witness, Marlene Tucker was still alive at a quarter past four.

What witness — or am I not allowed to ask?

Miss Brewis.

Lady Stubbs asked her to take down a tray to the young girl.

I don't believe that! Lady Stubbs' mind revolves entirely around herself.

What do you think of Lady Stubbs? Apparently she's mentally not very active?

I wouldn't describe her as an intellectual, no. But I'd say she's very much all there. For some reason she likes pretending to be the dim nitwit.

Where were you between four and five o'clock?

Well...

I can't really say off-hand. I was about, here and there.

I wasn't expecting to see you here, Poirot

I find myself once more embroiled in a crime.

Lady Stubbs has disappeared. She isn't in the house. The grounds are currently being searched.

Can you go and find out when and where she was last seen.

A murder first ...

... and then a disappearance.

What do you think?

Anything could have happened...

But right now we're concerned with Marlene Tucker's murder as our priority.

Of course...

All the same, it's very strange. A plain and not very clever kid is found strangled and not a hint of a motive... and...

One must admit that life is full of surprises. I came to spend an afternoon with a little cousin — and what happens? First I am engulfed in a kind of carnival with coconuts whizzing past my head, then immediately after, I am embroiled in a murder!

Oh dear, that Mrs Oliver has made me look at things differently with all the outlandish motives she suggested!

So, Mr De Sousa, you thought you would pay your cousin a surprise visit today?

Hardly a surprise visit, Inspector. I had already written to her.

30

I know that she received a letter from you this morning, but it was a surprise to her to know that you were in the country.

Oh, but you are wrong there, Inspector. I wrote to her... let me see, about three weeks ago.

You have not seen her since your arrival?

She seems to have gone missing.

Do you believe that she might have some reason for avoiding you?

What an absurd idea!

I have had no communication with her since she was a child. Why would she wish to avoid me?

Still searching the grounds, sir.

She hasn't gone out through the gate, the gardener who was giving out the tickets swears he hasn't seen her, as does the old boy Merdell down by the ferry.

31

31

Might she have slipped under a fence and gone off across country?

Yes, but she's wearing a crepe georgette dress, a large black hat and shoes with four-inch french heels.

Where's Hattie? You've got to do something!

This confounded fête has allowed some ruddy homicidal maniac to spend his afternoon going around murdering people!

Somebody ought to have noticed that Hattie disappeared...

Amanda, you were meant to be keeping an eye on things!

I can't be everywhere at once. If Lady Stubbs chose to wander away —

Wander away? Why would she?

Unless she wanted to avoid *that* fellow.

Why do you think she dreaded seeing her cousin so much?

Blessed if I really know...

She just kept saying that he was wicked. Maybe she heard him being talked about when she was a child and picked up odds and ends about him, had a sort of childish fear of him as a result. My wife can be rather childish sometimes.

What did she say exactly?

I...

I wouldn't want to go by — er — what she said...

She said, "He kills people."

I am devoted to my wife but half the time I don't listen to what she says as it doesn't make sense.

Anyway, this De Sousa fellow couldn't have had anything to do with this. Don't tell me he lands here off a yacht goes through the woods and kills a wretched Girl Guide! Why would he?

Lady Stubbs?

Oh yes, she's a bit strange up top, you know.

Where were you between four and five o'clock, Mrs Legge?

I went and had tea at four o'clock.

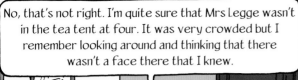

No, that's not right. I'm quite sure that Mrs Legge wasn't in the tea tent at four. It was very crowded but I remember looking around and thinking that there wasn't a face there that I knew.

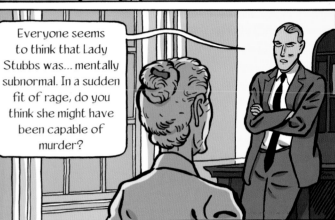

Everyone seems to think that Lady Stubbs was... mentally subnormal. In a sudden fit of rage, do you think she might have been capable of murder?

I won't allow you to say such things. Hattie was a gentle, warm-hearted girl.

Mrs Folliat, do you think that Lady Stubbs is dead?

I'm sure of it.

Good morning, Monsieur Weyman.

Dreadful atmosphere!

Never know what women get into their heads, or what fool thing they're likely to do!

I bet you agree with me, don't you Poirot?

Women are incalculable.

It's not as though we'd had words or a quarrel of any kind. But then she went off without a word!

There are some letters...

How the devil can I even think about business!

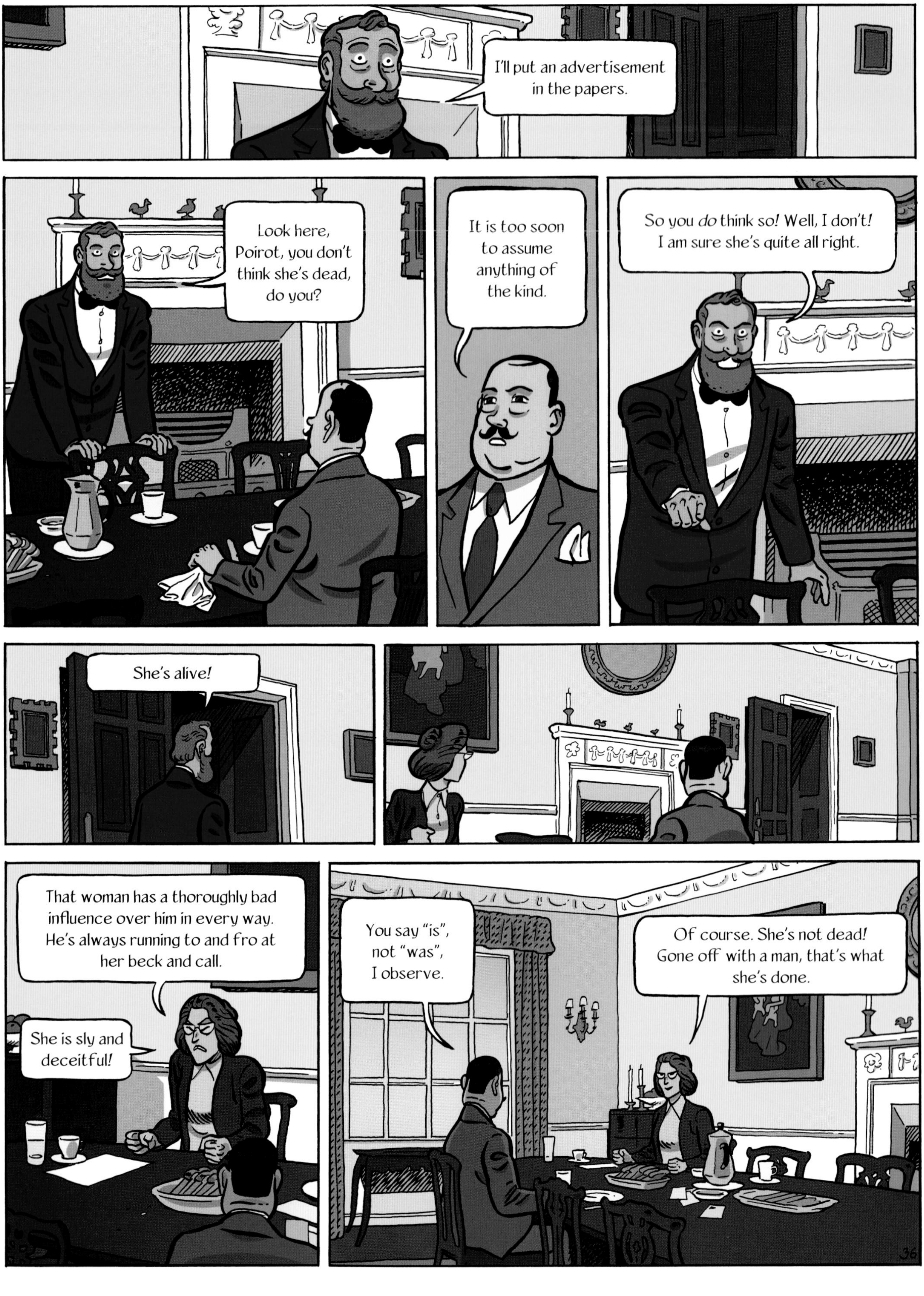
I'll put an advertisement in the papers.
Look here, Poirot, you don't think she's dead, do you?
It is too soon to assume anything of the kind.
So you *do* think so! Well, I don't! I am sure she's quite all right.
She's alive!
That woman has a thoroughly bad influence over him in every way. He's always running to and fro at her beck and call.
She is sly and deceitful!
You say "is", not "was", I observe.
Of course. She's not dead! Gone off with a man, that's what she's done.
36

This must be Lady Stubbs' hat...

Interesting! I hadn't noticed this little summer house before.

A woman's footsteps.

Nothing strange about that.

Everything has been left as it was.

But...

These must be the comics they gave her to keep her entertained..

Jackie Blakes goes with Susan
Georgie Porgie kisses hikers in the wood.

POIROT REMEMBERED MARLENE'S PLAIN, RATHER SPOTTY FACE. THE FRUSTRATED GIRL HAD SPIED AND SNOOPED ON OTHERS.

Perhaps she had seen something that she was not meant to have seen...?

I feel sure something is missing.

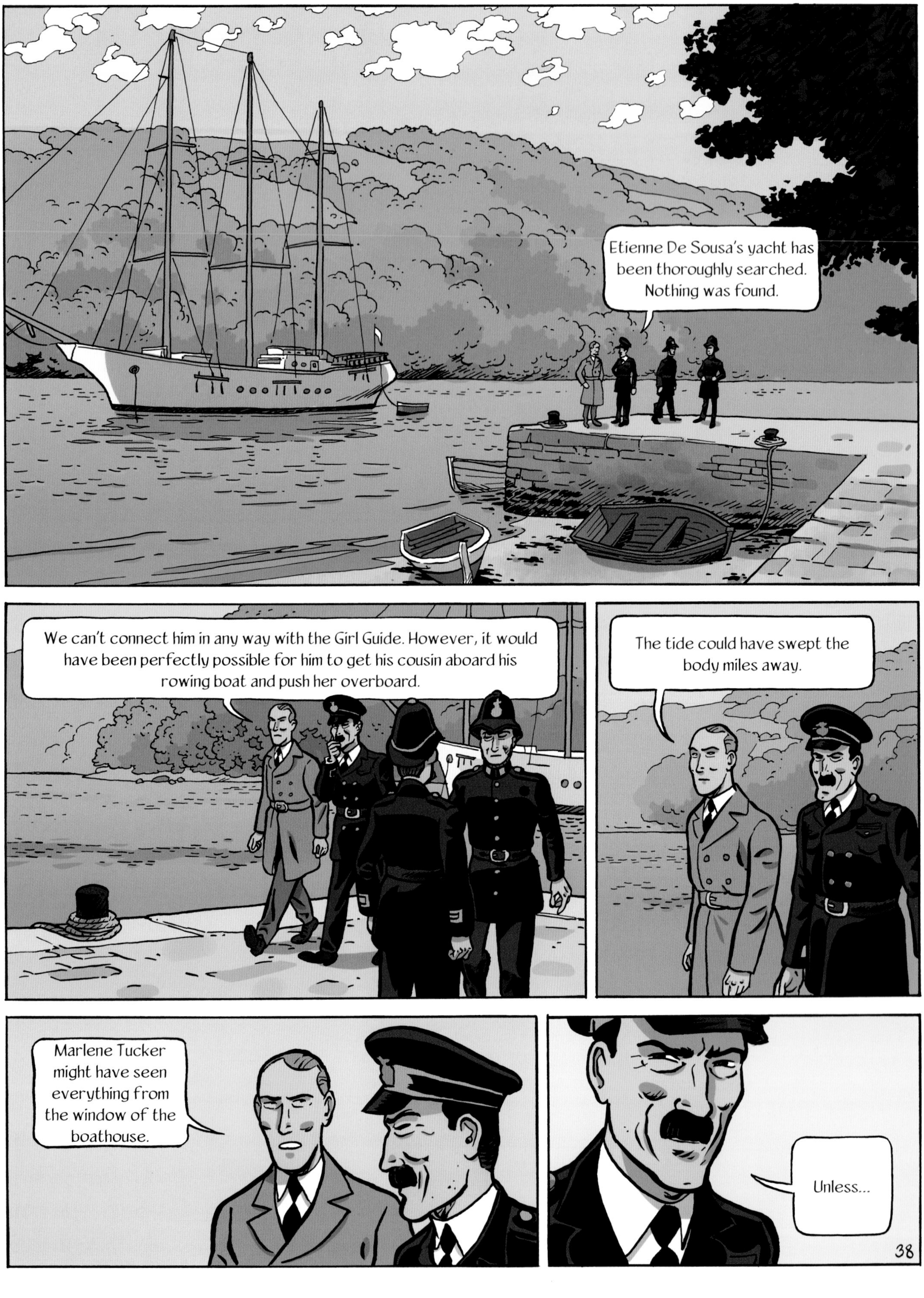
Etienne De Sousa's yacht has been thoroughly searched. Nothing was found.
We can't connect him in any way with the Girl Guide. However, it would have been perfectly possible for him to get his cousin aboard his rowing boat and push her overboard.
The tide could have swept the body miles away.
Marlene Tucker might have seen everything from the window of the boathouse.
Unless...
38

Unless Lady Stubbs was trying to run away from her husband and De Sousa was helping her.

Mrs Legge, Miss Brewis and Michael Weyman have given us unconvincing alibis.

So there are a number of possible suspects?

Far too many.

If only I knew what to look for!

Yes...

That is what I must do. The unlikely piece here, the improbable piece there...

Isolate the important details.

Mrs Folliat...

Now there is someone who knows more than she is willing to say...

POIROT WENT TO SEE MARLENE TUCKER'S PARENTS. THEY TOLD HIM OLD MERDELL HAD DIED. HIS BOAT WAS FOUND EMPTY AND THEY FISHED HIS BODY OUT OF THE RIVER SOME TIME LATER.

HE WAS ON THE WAY BACK FROM THE PUB AND HE MUST HAVE MISSED HIS FOOTING ON THE QUAY.

THE VERDICT WAS ACCIDENTAL DEATH.

My daughter dies, then my father goes as well!

You mean, Mrs Tucker, that Merdell was your father?

I have been very foolish. I have looked at everything the wrong way round!

Hi — mister.

I heard you talking with Mum. Marlene told me a secret.

Mum doesn't know, but Marlene used to get given money.

Money? From whom?

40

Someone at the house. But it's a secret!

I see, I see.

Mrs Oliver? I am so sorry to bother you whilst you are writing...

Did you, when you first began to plan your Murder Hunt, mean for the body to be in the boathouse?

Yes, I see...

Ah, very interesting.

I beg your pardon? A rucksack?!

CLICK

Of course!

The different pieces are now fitting together like in the jigsaw puzzle.

41

Lady Stubbs' body?!

I know where it is hidden. When we have found it, then you will have all the evidence you need. For only one person could have hidden it there.

Who's that?

As is so often the case, the husband. Sir George Stubbs.

But that's *impossible!* You know that!

You gave me a *fright!* I didn't see you coming.

I needed to know where you were between four and five on the day of the fair, Mrs Legge...

It was to see Michael Weyman, wasn't it?

That's all in the past now.

M. Poirot? Why have you come?

I think you can guess, madame...

There have been three deaths. Lady Stubbs, Marlene Tucker, old Merdell.

Merdell? That was an accident...

Oh, no...

Old Merdell recognized that Sir George Stubbs...

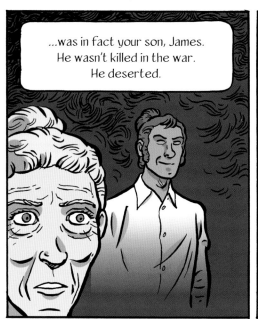

...was in fact your son, James. He wasn't killed in the war. He deserted.

You had the charge of a young girl, a subnormal but very rich girl, a certain Hattie...

By marrying her, your son became very rich. She signed everything he asked her to sign and he seized all her wealth.

43

A year ago, a Sir George Stubbs bought Nasse House and moved in.

James had aged and now had a beard. No-one apart from old Merdell recognized him. Merdell said to me that there would always be Folliats at Nasse House.

What you didn't know was that your son had already married in Trieste, a girl of the underground criminal world.

That first evening at Nasse House, George murdered young Hattie.

The next morning, the servants were introduced to "Hattie", who was actually his Italian wife.

You were very fond of poor Hattie Stubbs. When you spoke to me about her, in the past tense, you were talking about the *real* Hattie.

But then a totally unforeseen thing happened. One of real Hattie's cousins wrote to say that he was coming to England on a yachting trip. He hadn't seen Hattie for years but it was unlikely that he would have been deceived by the imposter...

There was an added complication. Old Merdell saw James burying Hattie.

He told his grand-daughter, Marlene, who then dropped hints to Sir George. He handed her small sums of hush money, and proceeded to make his plans.

George Stubbs fixed the date of the fête to coincide with De Sousa's arrival. Marlene Tucker would be killed and Lady Stubbs would disappear.

NASSECOMBE SUMMER FÊTE

On the day of the fête, Lady Stubbs had a "headache" and, dressed as an Italian tourist, checked in at the hostel.

YOUTH HOSTEL

She then managed to stage an appearance as a "trespasser" rebuffed by Sir George from the window of his wife's bedroom.

That afternoon, she came out wearing an elaborate dress, with shorts and a shirt under it. She told Miss Brewis to take a tea-tray down to Marlene.

This was to get her out of the way.

She quickly changed in the old summer-house that is hidden away in the shrubbery.

45

Shortly afterwards, she slipped down to the boathouse and strangled Marlene...

...before mingling with the crowd at the fête, masquerading as a tourist.

She spent the night at the Youth Hostel and left by bus the following morning. The police aren't looking for an Italian girl. They are looking for a simple, subnormal, exotic young woman wearing a dress and large hat.

Do not imagine I have no sympathy for you, madame. You can have no illusions about your son, but he was your son, and so you loved him.

Listen, can you hear? The blows of a pick axe...

They are breaking up the concrete foundation of the Folly...

Such a good place to hide a body...

THE END

46

Marek 2011